W9-CHJ-889

I Love Skating!

HAMILTON NORTH
PUBLIC LIBRARY
209 W. BRINTON ST.
CICERO, IN 46034

By Jane Feldman

A Random House PICTUREBACK® Book

Random House 🏠 New York

Copyright © 2002 by Jane Feldman. All rights reserved under International and Pan-American Copyright
Conventions. Published in the United States by Random House, Inc., New York, and simultaneously in
Canada by Random House of Canada Limited, Toronto.

PICTUREBACK, RANDOM HOUSE and colophon, and PLEASE READ TO ME and colophon are
registered trademarks of Random House, Inc.

Library of Congress Control Number: 2001089278   ISBN: 0-375-81341-1

Printed in the United States of America   First Edition   January 2002   10 9 8 7 6 5 4 3 2 1

www.randomhouse.com/kids

Hi! My name is Nastia.
I'm five years old, and
I love ice-skating!

I've been skating since I was only two.

My mom and dad are also skaters. They used to win medals when they competed in Russia. Then they moved to the United States and had me. Now they're both coaches.

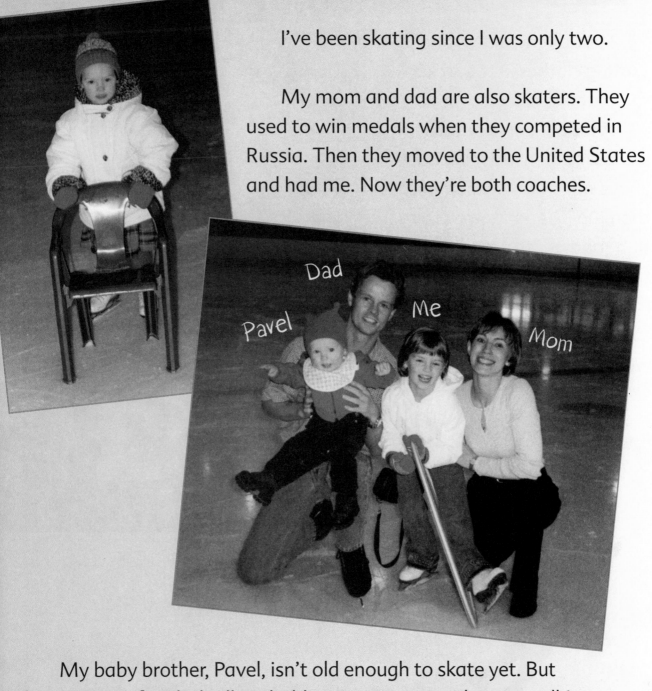

My baby brother, Pavel, isn't old enough to skate yet. But knowing my family, he'll probably start as soon as he can walk!

I put on my skates and skating clothes in the locker room at the rink.

A lot of people rent their skates, but I'm lucky because I have my own. My mom laces them up just right—not too tight and not too loose. If they're too tight, my feet might get numb. If they're too loose, my ankles will wobble and I could get hurt.

Boot

Blade

Outside edge

Inside edge

Guards

When I walk from the locker room to the ice, I wear guards over my blades. The guards make walking easier and keep the blades from getting dull.

SKATE HOUSE

I can hardly wait to start skating!

Brrr!

It's cold when I first
get on the ice.

But I warm up as soon as I start moving around.

The best part of skating is meeting other skaters. Sometimes I take group lessons at the rink where my parents coach. Group lessons are fun because everyone can help each other out.

When you're first learning to skate, it's a good idea to wear a helmet to protect your head.

I also meet people when I'm practicing.

This is my friend Ian. He plays hockey.

Here I am with my friend Joanie. She says that skating's fun at any age!

Uh-Oh!

The worst part of skating is falling down.

Ouch!

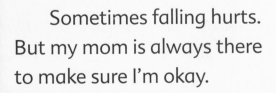

Sometimes falling hurts.
But my mom is always there
to make sure I'm okay.

I don't give up after a fall. I get right back up again.

As soon as I start skating,
I forget all about falling.

Ta-daa! Watch me!

This is called a spiral. A spiral is when you skate on one foot with the other leg pointed behind you. It looks like ballet.

Swish!

I'm doing a scratch spin. I spin around and around on one foot. I focus on one spot to help keep myself from getting dizzy. That's called spotting.

I can also do a dip. It's fun to see how low I can go.

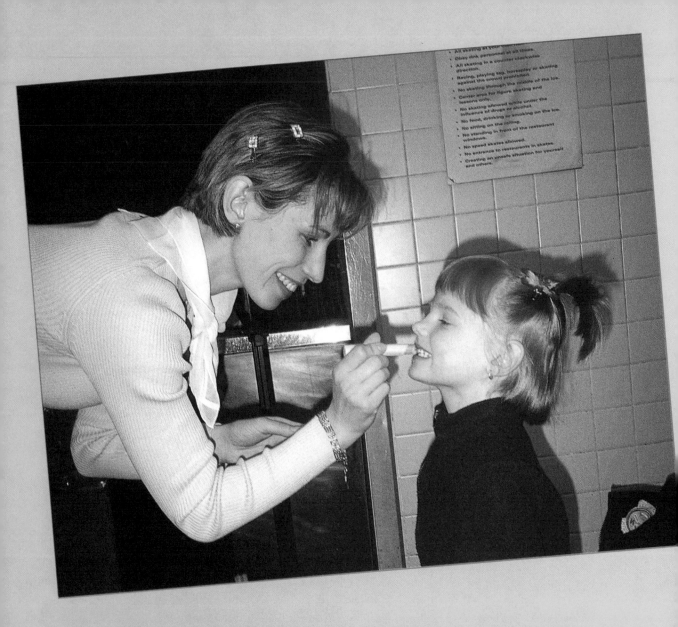

All the practicing I do pays off. This year, I entered my first competition. Getting ready was exciting. My mom even let me wear lip gloss.

I had to skate in front of judges, but I didn't get nervous. I just did my best and had fun, like I always do on the ice. After the competition, I won my very first trophy. I keep it in my room.

My friend Emily is twelve years old. Emily competes a lot and has <u>tons</u> of trophies and medals! She goes to the same rink I go to, and she says the only way to get better is to keep practicing.

Sometimes Emily helps me practice. She makes sure we sta with stretching to warm up our muscles so we won't get hurt.

Emily's been skating since she was younger than me, and she can do a lot of fancy moves. I can't do them all yet, so sometimes Emily helps spin me. It feels like I'm flying!

When the ice gets scratchy from everyone's blades, the Zamboni comes out and we have to take a break.

The Zamboni is a special machine that shaves off the top layer of ice. Then it washes the ice underneath and sprays hot water on it. The hot water melts the ice, and when it freezes again, there's a fresh, flat layer of ice to skate on.

I want the Zamboni to hurry up so we can get back out on the ice!

When we go back in the rink, the ice is smooth and we can skate really fast.

Emily is a great coach. She always tells me what we're going to work on and then helps me until I feel comfortable doing it on my own.

I love trying new moves. Her we are doing a shoot-the-duck. "Steady, Nastia," Emily says.

Before the rink closes, Emily and I practice doing curtsies. I curtsy at the end of all my routines. It's a way of saying "thank you" to whoever is watching.

I love skating!

At the end of the day, I don't want to leave the rink. The good news is, I know I'll be back tomorrow!